LEADING WHILE BLACK

LEADERSHIP STRATEGIES AND LESSONS
FOR TODAY'S BLACK PROFESSIONAL

MATTHEW R. DRAYTON

Leading While Black
Leadership Strategies and Lessons for Todays Black Professional
All Rights Reserved.
Copyright © 2021 Matthew R. Drayton
v3.0

The opinions expressed in this manuscript are solely the opinions of the author and do not represent the opinions or thoughts of the publisher. The author has represented and warranted full ownership and/or legal right to publish all the materials in this book.

This book may not be reproduced, transmitted, or stored in whole or in part by any means, including graphic, electronic, or mechanical without the express written consent of the publisher except in the case of brief quotations embodied in critical articles and reviews.

Outskirts Press, Inc.
http://www.outskirtspress.com

ISBN: 978-1-9772-2377-7

Cover Photo © 2021 www.gettyimages.com. All rights reserved - used with permission.

Outskirts Press and the "OP" logo are trademarks belonging to Outskirts Press, Inc.

PRINTED IN THE UNITED STATES OF AMERICA

Acknowledgments

I would like to thank God for looking over and blessing me throughout my life. I would also like to thank my late parents Matthew (Buddy) Drayton and Juanita Simmons Drayton. Mom, you left to soon, but the years I spent with you made a meaningful impact on my life. Dad, despite your flaws and personal struggles you were always there for me when Mom died, and you taught me how to be a man. I remember, love, and honor you both daily.

To my beautiful wife Lila, I would like to thank you for your support over the years. We make a great team, we raised a wonderful family and achieved more than we ever dreamed we could. I love you. To my daughters Tiffanie and Brittny, thanks for being there for me and for providing realness to my life that gave me purpose and has kept me grounded and focused. I am beyond proud of the women you both have become.

To Carl, my best friend from the old neighborhood, thanks for being a great friend all these years. To Danny, thanks for your friendship over the years; we have been through a lot together.

You have been like a brother to me. Thanks for being a sounding board. I would also like to thank the Drayton family, Davis family, Chisholm family, Brown family, Whiting family, Johnson family, Evans family, Strouse family, Dickens family, Haynes family, and Muldrow family for all their friendship, support, and counsel.

Lastly, thanks to the men and women I served with in the US Army, as a DoD civilian and everyone I worked with during my many career endeavors. There were so many of you who made an impact on my life; way too many to name. You helped me grow as a leader and as a man. I truly appreciate your friendship, guidance, and patience throughout the years.

Contents

Author's Foreword	i
1. What Is Leadership?	1
2. My Leadership Journey	7
3. Learning to Follow	22
4. Mentoring and Leadership	29
5. Leadership Challenges	37
6. Compassion and Leadership	44
7. Developing Teammates	49
8. Leading Upward	55
9. Networking for Success	59
10. Leading Future Generations	62
11. The Only Black in the Office	65
12. Effective Communication	69
13. Leadership and Activism	73
14. Toxic Leadership	76
15. The Talking Points Leader	80
16. Leadership and Self-Care	85
Summary	88

Author's Foreword

THIS IS MY second book that has the "While Black" phrase in the title. I learned a lot about public's perceptions of this phrase after my first book "Succeeding While Black" was published in 2013. Additionally, I received a lot of interesting feedback. I heard everything from "Succeeding While Black" was too focused on race, to I should have removed the "While Black" phrase from the title all together because of its negative implications.

There were some critics who felt I was alienating a large part of my potential audience and limiting book sales because the title targeted one demographic, African Americans. While there was some truth in most of the feedback I received, I stand by my decision to name my first book "Succeeding While Black" and I decided to use the "While Black" phrase again in the title of this book "Leading While Black."

I don't write to exclude anyone or for monetary gain. I write to help people, express ideas, entertain, and to provoke thought and discussion. As a mentor of African American youth, I realize we (African Americans) still need help in several areas of American society, especially leadership. As a people, we are falling by the wayside in many constructive statistical categories, while Black leaders struggle mightily with acceptance from their peers and with getting the respect they deserve from their subordinates.

I have experienced the joy, pain, and struggles of being African American in leadership positions. My hope is by sharing my experiences, I can help current and future Black leaders avoid some of the mistakes I made and mistakes I observed being made by other Black leaders during my career. What follows are my personal accounts of leadership, with a focus on African American leaders. I hope this book resonates, enlightens, and inspires all who read it to become better leaders, and reach their full leadership potential.

I am very fortunate to have served with and worked for some of the most charismatic, competent and effective leaders in the military and corporate sectors. I also consider it a blessing to have worked with, and for, some of the worst. Both have afforded me a rare opportunity to see leadership from many perspectives. I do not name any of those leaders in this book; I don't feel it's necessary. However, I do talk about and cite examples of leaders from my extensive military and corporate career.

Growing up as a poor Black male in Georgia, there were lessons and examples of leadership all around me. That was and is my foundation. The day that changed my life forever was the day I walked into an Army recruiting office. I knew the Army would be tough, but I had to do something different and change my circumstances. Little did I know my career would span nearly three decades, and I would retire at the highest enlisted rank of sergeant major.

The military taught me discipline, work ethic, provided me a formal education and the opportunity to travel all over the world. However, the thing I am most thankful for is the leadership training and lessons I learned while serving my country—lessons and stories I will share with you in hope that they will help you become a better leader, too.

The best education and leadership training in the world will not help you if you don't apply it properly and listen to what others have to say (verbal and nonverbal). I have personally witnessed graduates from the nation's most prestigious military academies and academic institutions who were inept, incapable, and ineffective as leaders.

Those leaders struggled primarily because they refused to recognize and accept input from others, and because they treated their team members poorly. I believe the way you treat people and how they respond to you is extremely important to being an effective leader. Most people can tell within a minute of meeting and talking with you if you care about them or not, and if you are sincere.

Why write a book about Black leadership? Because I and many Black leaders I know faced unique challenges and struggled mightily as African Americans in leadership roles. Additionally, I watched Black leaders struggle at every level in leadership roles during my career. I wrote this book with the intent to address African American leadership, and the unique challenges we face.

Leadership truly starts at home, with the raising of our children.

That is the first opportunity to instill discipline, a primary component of leadership and success. We must refocus our children toward higher education, good work ethic, good morals, and doing what's right. We need to encourage them to succeed. Leaders, both effective and ineffective, are cultivated through example.

Setting good examples for our children will grow worthy African American leaders of the future. African Americans in leadership roles will face numerous challenges and will be judged by a different set of standards; we will have to fight and work harder than our peers. That is how it is and how it will be, but being a leader is worth every struggle, because there is no greater feeling than motivating, developing, and helping others…that's what great leaders do, regardless of race or ethnicity. Embrace your leadership role; you were chosen for a reason.

Chapter 1

What Is Leadership?

The million-dollar question. Leadership has different meanings to many different individuals and organizations. Leadership is a popular and relentless topic of discussion in the workplace and in our private lives. Leadership influences important aspects of our lives every day. The impacts of leadership can affect our success as a person, a family, a business or organization, and as a nation.

My definition of leadership is taking responsibility for what needs to be done and influencing and empowering others to get it done to acceptable completion while avoiding problems and making people around you better all at the same time.

Leadership is about making very hard decisions and being able to live with them regardless of the outcome of the decision. Most importantly, leadership is about doing what's right and taking care of the people you lead and your organization. Leadership is not about the leader.

I believe leadership, or the lack thereof, is the leading cause of most of the problems the world faces today. From the many financial crises in the world, to pandemics, environmental issues and corruption, and the political chaos in Washington D.C., leadership plays a vital part in everything that impacts our way of life.

As leaders, we are responsible for developing team members and identifying those team members with the potential for advancement, and those with the potential to be our successors. Members of your team are not there for your entertainment, to be hazed or abused, or to support personal agendas.

During my career, I witnessed countless leaders abuse their power, creating toxic work environments all while stifling productivity and individual initiative. They cost their organizations revenue and team member retention and caused a decline in morale and efficiency. Leadership is a delicate balance between being stern and forceful, and being compassionate and understanding.

Many in leadership roles are reluctant to lead or be innovative, because they are ill prepared, or lack the proper training, courage, and discipline to do so. Then there are those who want to lead for all the wrong reasons; they seek leadership roles for fame, fortune, or hidden agendas.

Leadership requires strength and courage, and leadership requires persons who are willing to be fair and firm, take risks, and most importantly, do what is right. It cannot be stressed enough how important doing what's right is. Leaders must also make major sacrifices and make decisions that they know will not always be popular.

Leading people and being operationally responsible for organizations are not easy tasks, especially for African Americans and other minorities. African American and minority leaders face a different set of hurdles as leaders in every occupation, particularly in the corporate world. What follows are examples and opinions based on my experiences as an African American leader in the military, corporate, and government sectors.

Leadership has nothing to do with position or title. I have worked for many senior people with titles, seniority, and positions that were dreadful leaders. Leadership has nothing to do with personal qualities. Most think of charismatic leaders like General Powell or Dr. King when we think of great Black leaders. Leadership isn't always about being outgoing and demonstrative; I have worked for great leaders who were soft spoken, and quite unassuming.

Leadership is often confused with management. Leadership and management are not the same. Leaders have vision and influence and inspire others to follow them through their acts and deeds. Managers execute the leader's vision. Managers must be able to plan, coordinate, and solve day-to-day problems in their organizations.

I believe leadership begins in the home. Many minorities still cope with inequalities in every aspect of their lives; however, we cannot ignore the lack of leadership in our homes and in our communities, when it comes to education, crime, and violence. By teaching our children at an early age through positive example, we prepare them to be leaders of the future.

Leadership is not only about telling people what to do or following orders. Leadership is about discipline, accountability, and setting a positive example for your team to follow. Everything else will take care of itself. This applies to any leader, regardless of race or gender.

Ask a group of leaders their definition of leadership, and you will get different answers and opinions. With these differing opinions, it's pretty clear there is not a single definition of leadership. Much of what we know about leadership comes from history and our experiences with success and failure. What works for one leader may not necessarily work for another, depending on the circumstances. However, a good leader has to be able to inspire and influence people.

Leadership in the Black community has evolved over the years. There are obstacles and apathy in many areas of our community: employment, education, voting, academics, and economic accountability. Social media protest has replaced the type of activism that brought about the changes during the civil rights movement. Very few Black leaders are willing to take risks and address the many issues facing the African American community. When we speak to Black leadership, we are addressing most of the issues facing Black people, because the lack of leadership is where many of the problems in our communities start.

Throughout my career I have faced many leadership challenges. I have had some degree of success, and I have had more than my share of failures. I have worked for some of the best leaders in America. I have also worked for some of the worst. I will occasionally reference leaders from my past, but not by name because their names aren't what's important, their actions are.

Disagreements with my opinions are expected. My views on leadership come from forty years' work and leadership experience as a Black man and are intended to provoke a civil conversation. Not a word in this book was written out of anger, bitterness, or with an agenda.

This book was written to help Black leaders better understand the challenges they face and provide strategies to help them better navigate through their leadership journeys. Many of the strategies in this book can be applied by anyone in a leadership role regardless of their race. I welcome different perspectives and feedback on Black leadership, and I realize other Black leaders have been through different experiences on their leadership journeys.

I am blessed to have been exposed to and worked for so many great leaders over the years. My military and government jobs allowed me to work for and with leaders from many ethnicities. II have also had personal access to senior military, government, and corporate leaders that many of my Black peers and subordinates did not have access to. They shared information and experiences with me that changed my life. That is why I feel uniquely qualified to write about Black leadership.

I am at an age where I am closer to the end than I am the beginning, and I truly appreciate things more. I have a great life and I owe it all to opportunities and the leaders and leadership I've been exposed to (positive and negative). I feel an obligation to share the leadership lessons that I have learned. My hope is there is something in this book that will resonate and help African American leaders (especially the youth) while on their journey. We have a responsibility to provide for our young.

Chapter 2

My Leadership Journey

Are people born leaders, are they developed and made, or is it a combination of the two? I read an article in *Entrepreneur* magazine by Lewis Howes about born leadership. Howes makes the argument that we are all born leaders, because being responsible for your life and making tough life decisions on a daily basis is a form of leadership. While I somewhat agree with Howe's opinion, I also believe that leadership and being a great leader goes beyond making life decisions. Leadership primarily focuses on leading and influencing others. It's about pushing yourself beyond the things you normally do. Leadership is taking on more responsibility and doing things others don't want to do and making the hard decisions others don't want to make.

Although I was fairly confident as a child, I did not consider myself a born leader. I had a hard time following orders and was rebellious, like most young boys. In elementary school I would never volunteer to read aloud and would try to avoid going to the blackboard or situations where I had to speak in front of the class.

When I arrived at junior high school, I had lost some of my shyness, but was still struggling with being disciplined and following orders. I remember struggling with retaining information and focusing on my lessons. During high school, I focused enough to graduate, but I didn't excel at anything and I really admired my classmates who served on school clubs, committees, and those who held senior class offices.

After I graduated from high school, I worked in the grocery business and waited tables in my hometown, Savannah, Georgia while living at home with my father. I badly wanted to go to college, but we couldn't afford tuition and my grades were not good enough to be considered for scholarships. It became very clear that I did not prepare myself for life after high school or as an adult.

I made somewhat decent money busing and waiting tables. I also had my initial introductions to leadership from the many supervisors and managers I had at different jobs. The first Black leader I ever worked for was Mr. Richardson at M&M Supermarkets. Mr. Richardson was a well-dressed man who always wore a crisp shirt and tie.

Mr. Richardson was very articulate, competent, and soft spoken. What stood out most to me was how much all of the team members and customers liked and respected him. Growing up, there were not many Black men with white-collar management jobs in my neighborhood, so I really looked up to him. I would pick Mr. Richardson's brain as often as he would allow me to.

I dreamed of having a job where I could wear a suit, or shirt and tie, one day. But how could I do that without a college degree? I left M&M to work at several upscale restaurants, but I never worked for another Black manager or supervisor again. Looking back, I realize now that M&M Supermarkets were way ahead of their time with regard to hiring. I never forgot Mr. Richardson. He definitely made an impact on me, one that lasts to this day.

I enjoyed earning my own money and had fun learning about food and wine and learning about business in general. However, I quickly got bored with those jobs, and I felt there was a big world out there that I wanted to see. There was more out there I wanted to do!

I was lying in my bedroom staring at an Eagles album cover (Hotel California) mural I painted on my wall, thinking about my future, and how unprepared for adult life I was. I kept thinking there had to be something better than what I was doing. Where should I start?

After mulling over my few options, I started thinking about a career in the military. I had seen a few people from my neighborhood achieve success in the military. I also saw some of my neighbors' military careers end in failure. This was a big decision, but it was one I had to make alone. Looking back on it, the decision to go in the military may have been one of my first big leadership tests.

While returning from a run on a hot humid day in June, I walked into the Army recruiter's office—a decision that changed my life forever! The recruiter was a tall Black sergeant who looked really good in his uniform. He welcomed me in and pulled my ASVAB (test) scores. These were my results from the military entry test I had taken in high school. As he started telling me which jobs I qualified for, I quickly realized I should have taken those military aptitude test I took in high school more seriously. I was unqualified for many of the Army jobs I sought because my test scores were pretty low (I did retake and raise them later). I had no intention of joining the Army, so I basically blew those tests off; I didn't even finish them. Leadership lesson one: Do your best on every exam, test, or challenge regardless of your interest or future intentions.

Staff Sergeant West, a tall Black soldier with a commanding presence, welcomed me in, said a few words, and before I knew it, I had signed up. I walked out of that recruiting office a future soldier. I don't know if it was the uniform SSG West was wearing or the convincing words he spoke to me, but I had made a decision that would change my life forever. I didn't discuss enlisting in the military with my father or anyone else. I just did it!

I am so meticulous and detail-oriented now, it is still hard for me to believe I walked into that recruiter's office without a plan, but I was very young then. When I told my father that I joined the Army, he was not thrilled. I think he felt like he was betrayed, and in hindsight I regret not telling him, but it was a spontaneous decision. My decision to join the Army had no malicious intent.

I recommend that anyone who is considering a military career (or any career) do research prior to committing. Never walk into a recruiter's office or any situation unprepared and without a plan like I did. I could have gotten a much better assignment had I researched it, but I have no regrets about how my military career, or my life to this point, turned out. I am beyond blessed.

I did well enough to get in the Army. I just didn't qualify for some of the more technical jobs the Army had to offer. Logistics was the most appealing job the recruiter had available, and I was ready to leave Savannah, so I signed up. I remember walking home from the recruiter's office stunned. I had done it; I signed up to join the United States Army.

I was leaving for Fort Jackson, South Carolina in two weeks to take a physical and in-process into the military. If that went well, I would go to basic combat training in January of the upcoming year. I boarded a bus to Columbia, South Carolina to take a military physical and be sworn into the military. There were dozens of us teenagers getting poked and prodded by military doctors. If there was something medically wrong with you, those doctors were going to find it. There were many recruits who were not allowed to join the Army because of medical conditions that were discovered by the doctors during our physicals.

After all the test and interviews were complete, those of us who were fit enough were taken into a brightly lit room with a big American flag, where we raised our right hands and took an oath to protect and defend the United States of America. We were now soldiers! When I returned from my military physical and in-processing, I was officially in the Army with a reporting date to begin basic combat training, and advanced individual training.

I had five months to prepare before I departed for Army basic training. I didn't know it at the time, but I would never live full time in Savannah again. I was excited and anxious at the same time—what had I done? I wanted to leave home and see other parts of the world, but there was a part of me that wondered if I had I made the right decision. Seeing my friends join and serve in the military was one thing; me serving in uniform myself was another. There was excitement, apprehension, and doubt. I spent those five months working as a waiter, working out, and getting in shape for the military. I started to feel a little guilty about leaving my father in Savannah by himself. He had been there for me when my mom died, and now I was leaving him at home alone. That was something I really struggled with then and sometimes even now.

Five months flew by quickly; before I knew it, I had a few weeks before I reported for basic combat training. I wish, I had spent more time with my father before I left, but we did not have the type of relationship where either of us expressed feelings. My dad was old school, and showing of affection was seen as being weak. I told myself if I ever became a father, I never wanted to have that type of relationship with my children.

Nothing can really prepare a young person for joining the military; there are too many unknowns. I didn't have access to ROTC. I had friends and family who served that give me tips and information, but I know now that everyone's military experience is different. I worked out and ran a lot while I was at home, so I would be in decent shape when I arrived at basic combat training. But other than knowing I had to be physically fit, I had no Idea what to expect.

As the days started to get closer to my departure, I realized that my life was going to change forever. I was going away, into the Army. I was going to be on my own for the first time. This would be my first leadership test.

I spent my last night at home on Savannah beach. It was a cold, clear night in January; it was way too cold to be on the beach, but I knew it would be a while before I would be able go to the beach again. I sat and talked with my girlfriend as the tides came in and out. I had only a few hours left as a civilian.

The next day my father took me to the Greyhound bus station. He gave me the usual warnings about behaving and avoiding trouble. We shook hands, and I boarded the bus for what turned out to be a two-and-a-half-decade journey that would carry me all over the world. Nothing I would do for the rest of my life would change me (for the better) like joining the Army did.

We were met at the bus station by military personnel and transferred to an Army bus. When that bus pulled into the Fort Jackson, SC basic training area, I started to hear loud noises, which sounded like voices and chaos. As we got closer the noises got louder, the next thing I knew a drill sergeant was beating on the bus window, yelling for us to get off the bus. As soon as we got off the bus, the drill sergeant made us do jumping jacks and pushups until exhaustion. What in the world had I gotten myself into?

As I did jumping jacks and pushups on that cold January ground in South Carolina I felt I had made a mistake—I thought then the biggest mistake of my life. The recruiter told me I could learn a trade get money for college and travel the world, but he didn't mention anything about doing exercises and being yelled at in the freezing cold.

The drill sergeant was a tall muscular Black man with a booming voice and a death stare. "Look at all you maggots; you came here to ruin my Army," he said. "Well, I'm not going to let that happen. I'm going to make every one of you quit," the drill sergeant said. "Does anyone want to quit right now?" I thought about how different this Black leader was from Mr. Richardson at M&M supermarket.

As I stood there sweating in the winter cold from what seemed like hours of physical training (PT), I thought really hard about quitting. The yelling, the physical training; maybe the Army wasn't for me. I could always go back to Georgia and find a job. But something deep inside told me I had to stick it out. I could not go home after only one day because I was yelled at and made to do pushups; I couldn't go back to Waldburg street as a quitter, but more importantly I could not let my father down. I could not face him, especially if I quit. This was another important leadership lesson. Even though I was very young, I realized you must finish what you start. You can't quit just because you face adversity.

I decided that the only way I was going home without graduating was if the Army sent me home for some reason. I vowed I would not quit no matter how hard it got, and it did get extremely hard. Basic combat training was very different from what it is now. drill sergeants could do basically anything they wanted to you!

Waking up every morning at 3 a.m., then doing physical training in freezing weather, was tough on all of us recruits. After physical training we would conduct basic combat training all day. An average training day lasted around seventeen hours. The highlights of the day were the three meals we were served daily; however, we had about five minutes to eat them, and no talking!

The drill sergeant's job was to mold teenage civilians into combat trained soldiers in eight weeks. Not an easy task. My drill sergeants' last names were Chambers and Alvin. Their first names were drill sergeant. Both were Black males, both were tough, and both were physical specimens.

Chambers was six feet tall and stood erect like he owned the world. Alvin was about six feet four inches tall and walked with a certain swagger. Whenever we marched by female recruits, they always paid Drill Sergeant Alvin a lot of attention. These two men and my classmates were the only family I had for eight weeks. By the way, my first name became "trainee"—so did all the other recruits.

So, we went on training day after day, week after week…marching, running, shooting, and learning. The more I trained, the better I became at soldiering. I was starting to catch on to things and I realized that if I did things better than most of my peers, the drill sergeants would leave me alone and focus on (yell at) the trainees who needed more help or were struggling. So, I worked hard on being above average, a trait all successful leaders must possess.

Basic training was going smooth until that one evening in the barracks. There was a trainee from Chicago named PVT Bodley. He was a loudmouth know it all who was not liked by most of the other recruits. He would regularly bully trainees in the barracks after the drill sergeants left for the night. On this particular night he came up to me wanting to pick a fight, and I was in no mood for it. We started fighting, and soon it looked like a scene out of a movie—trainees yelling, furniture moving, and things breaking. It got really ugly. Next thing I knew, a hand was grabbing me by my shirt behind my neck. It was Drill Sergeant Chambers, and he was not happy.

He took both of us to his office and said he was going to send both of us home right then. After six weeks of hard training, I had thrown it all away because I wasn't smart or disciplined enough to walk away from a fight. How could I be so stupid? When Drill Sergeant Chambers called me in his office, I started to cry. I told him this was not the way I wanted to go home, for something as stupid as fighting. After all, I joined the Army to get away from all that.

I promised him that if he gave me another chance, I would prove to him that I could be a soldier. I begged him. As I stood there awaiting his verdict, I realized this must be what it's like to stand in front of a judge.

When Drill Sergeant chambers began to speak, I was extremely nervous. He said, "Boy, I'm going to let you stay, but if you get into any more trouble, I will send your butt home so quick you won't know what hit you." Whew, I had dodged a bullet and gotten a second chance to stay in the Army.

After the fight, I knew I could not afford to mess up again. From that point on, I did everything I was told, and I studied hard to become a good soldier. I graduated from basic combat training in March with a certificate for superior performance. This was the first time I had achieved anything as an adult.

I felt lean, mean, and strong. I had completed the toughest challenge in my life. I wished my father could have come to see me graduate, but he never traveled much. As me and my classmates waited for our orders to our next assignment, I had no idea what was in store for me after basic training, but I knew whatever it was, I felt I was prepared for it.

During basic training, I had to give everything I had physically and mentally for those eight weeks. I was reprogramed to function like as disciplined soldier. There were many of my fellow classmates (more than 100) who could not handle the stress and rigorous physical and mental training; they were sent home.

I did not know it at the time, but basic combat training (BCT) prepared me leadershipwise more than anything else I had done up to that point in my life. Drill Sergeants Chambers and Alvin joined Mr. Richardson as Black leaders who had impacted my life and my thoughts on leadership in a very positive way.

Some of the leadership lessons I learned in BCT have stayed with me for life; I had the good fortune to serve in the US Army for twenty-six years, working with and providing vital support to our nation's heroes.

When I joined the Army, Jimmy Carter was President of the United States. The Viet Nam war had recently ended but, there were still remnants of that war around the late '70s and '80s. The Army had many leaders during that period that were not equipped to lead men because they were drafted (involuntarily) into the military, and many of them (feeling forced) had no desire to serve.

My first platoon sergeant in the US Army was almost functionally illiterate. He had trouble expressing himself and communicating effectively both written and orally. He was not alone; the war had produced a lot of individuals who were in leadership positions that had Post Traumatic Stress Disorder (PTSD) and other illnesses. As a result, some young Black soldiers had very few positive African American role models and mentors as leaders to look up to and emulate.

My leadership journey was an accidental one. I never intended to make the Army a career. I wanted to get away from home, earn some money, and travel. Initially I didn't pay too much attention to the leaders in my chain of command because most of them were nothing special, and they only barked out orders while doing very little mentoring or teaching. However, my mind started to change about the military once I got an assignment in Germany.

Before I knew it, I had served ten years, gotten married, and fathered two children. I had become a career soldier and I was really enjoying what I was doing and getting promoted slightly ahead of schedule. I was also observing and learning different leadership styles and lessons, while also learning what to do and not to do as a leader.

In November of 1987, something happened that changed my Army career and my life. I was a platoon sergeant at Fort Bragg North Carolina, having a fairly ordinary day when two men from the US Special Operations Command came to my office looking to recruit me for a special assignment. I was very skeptical of these two men, but I decided to listen to their pitch. They were somewhat goofy, and I really didn't believe they were from where they said they were from. However, they were convincing enough to get me to submit a hiring packet to join US Army Special Operations.

I was at the ten-year mark in the Army, which meant I had ten years to go before I was eligible for retirement at twenty years. I was a staff sergeant who was considering submitting a warrant officer application packet. I had spent my entire career serving in conventional military forces and was about to embark on a journey that would change my thought process and how I viewed leadership forever.

After numerous interviews, psychological exams, physical fitness and swim tests, I was selected to serve with United States Special Operations Forces (SOF). I struggled initially with the way business was done in the SOF community. I was used to being told exactly what to do and telling others exactly what to do when I served with conventional forces. In Special Operations you were given a job and left alone to do it, sometimes with very little direct supervision. This was foreign to me, but I realized that if I wanted to survive and be an effective leader, I would have to learn to adapt to the SOF way and change my way of thinking and doing business.

After serving in SOF a few years, I found myself traveling all over the world, sometimes alone, with large amounts of money and responsibility. I was given opportunities to represent SOF forces at the State Department, CIA, US Embassies abroad, and with law enforcement and other civilian and government agencies. This was very tricky work sometimes. You had to develop an understanding of non-military cultures, something I fortunately was able to grasp fairly quickly and something I put a lot of effort into. I did have a lot of help from great peers and leaders in the SOF community.

Working without someone watching you and not over-directing you is not the Army way. Neither is working with other government agencies. Some of my teammates struggled with the lack of oversight and direction and with working with civilian and non-DOD agencies.

One thing that really stood out when I arrived in the SOF community two decades ago was the scarcity of African American leaders. There were very few Black soldiers' in SOF, period, and those few who were there were not serving in leadership positions.

That has definitely changed over the years; however, most of the leaders I worked with and for in the SOF community were white. For the record, the majority of those white leaders were very good leaders and most treated me fairly. However, there were a few who didn't feel I belonged in SOF, and they let me know it through their actions.

I believe strong and weak leadership traits have very little to do with a leader's ethnicity. However, an ineffective Black leader will very likely be given less of a chance to succeed than a white colleague. I have seen this play out numerous times. In SOF and in other military and business sectors, the margin for error is vastly smaller for an African American in a leadership position compared to his Caucasian peers. This is something all African Americans who are given leadership roles need to understand and be prepared for.

I am truly blessed to have served with and under leaders who truly understood that our mission wasn't about them, but about making those around them better. I am also blessed to have had the opportunity to lead men and women, be responsible for millions of dollars' worth of equipment, and make major decisions. I am grateful for my military service. It was a leadership education like no other.

There were many leaders during my military and corporate careers who gave me opportunities and helped me become the man I am today. A few gave me opportunities when I didn't feel I deserved them. There are way too many people to name, but they know who they are, and I want them to know that I am eternally grateful for them taking a chance on me. I learned a lot about leadership along the way, and I owe it all to being given opportunities to lead, and more importantly, to make mistakes.

I have worked for and beside many great leaders; some of them are making headlines in the news and making history as leaders today. I have also worked for leaders who I felt needed vast improvement but were trying their best, and unfortunately, I have worked for leaders who were just totally inept. I learned from them all, and I hope some of my leadership experiences in the following chapters will benefit you.

Chapter 3

LEARNING TO FOLLOW

AMAZON HAS OVER 80,000 leadership books in their catalog. It is a popular topic, and one that garners a substantial volume of perspectives, advice, suggestions, and strategies. However, when it comes to leadership books about being an effective follower, Amazon has a little over 1,000 books. The disparity is glaring, and I get it that an entire book written about how to follow is a stretch, but it does show the lack of emphasis on being a good follower and its criticality to effective leadership.

I believe being a great leader is predicated on learning to become a good follower. Following leaders, instructions, and policies correctly requires a significant amount of discipline. Sometimes you have to do things a certain way when you know there are more efficient and sometimes better ways to do them, especially when team members are left alone without supervision.

I have worked with and for individuals who didn't listen to their subordinates, peers, or superiors in the workplace. They struggled mightily on their jobs and in their daily lives, to include their relationships, because they could not accept input from others. This behavior usually starts early with parents allowing a child to negotiate or dictate terms to them. Once this behavior is learned and established, it is very hard to correct.

A person simply cannot lead if they are incapable of following. Early in life, I too resented being told what to do by anyone, including my parents. There were a few people I respected—my coaches and a few of my teachers—but there was no one that I wanted to be led by or told by them how things should be done. I thought I had all of the answers.

I believe a good leader understands early on that without being able to follow, they will have trouble being effective and finding true success. As we educate and mentor future leaders, we must stress to them and show them by our example how important it is to be able to follow, which means listening to others and receiving feedback, even if it goes against your plans, goals, or objectives.

Today's leadership development focuses primarily on team members, managers, and leaders. During my career and currently, there is very little discussion or focus on how followership helps one to become a better leader.

There are certain traits and characteristics one must have to learn how to follow. Learning to follow requires humility, openness, and the ability to trust and accept input from others. It also requires you to be able to work well with and have respect for others; rarely will a person follow someone they don't respect. I once worked for a person who never took input from any of his subordinates;

in fact, he even rebelled against input from his leaders.

This leader created an extremely toxic environment, destroying morale, innovation, and creativity. Every idea, presentation, meeting, or product had to be produced by him. No one else on the team's input had any merit. It took years to undo and rebuild the troubled work environment he created.

This leader regularly commented about how his bosses were doing things wrong, and how they were not leading the organization correctly. This person could not follow, and it cost him severely when it came down to future assignments and promotions. As a leader, it is vital to stress how important learning to follow is to your entire team, and set the example by being a good follower yourself. If you have disagreements with your leadership, discuss it with them privately and never badmouth your superiors to your team, regardless of how upset you are.

I believe following begins with trust, being open to others, and being willing to accept their differences. Just because a person is different or has different views from us, that doesn't mean they are not worthy of being accepted as a leader. The only way to obtain the critical leadership skills we all need is by learning how to follow and model ourselves after others in leadership positions. This means learning what to do, and not to do, as a leader.

Following requires you to seek out mentors and effective leaders to learn from. It also requires you to observe and distinguish between effective and ineffective leadership. Ineffective leaders usually realize their shortcomings and overcompensate in various ways to hide them. Instead of creating productive work environment and mentoring their subordinates, they create an atmosphere of fear, avoidance, and chaos for their followers. Leaders need to remember that in most cases, their leadership example is the example being set for the next generation. Poor leaders create poor followers who go on to develop additional poor leaders, which can hamper organizational culture for years.

We should view the opportunity to follow as a privilege because it allows us to learn. Those that follow should consider their role as a follower an opportunity, a chance to greatly enhance their ability to lead. Instead of viewing the leader with disdain or as someone to be tolerated, try to learn everything you can (good or bad) from them. Even the most difficult of leaders can teach us something.

The ineffective and difficult leaders I worked for taught me just as much or more than the effective leaders I worked for. It is rare to go through an entire career and not experience working for an ineffective leader. Being fortunate enough to have good leaders and mentors can provide solid, positive direction for future leaders and propel them to success. Following a leader is not just an obligation required by contract; it is way to learn the critical leadership skills required to help you in your chosen career.

Being a good leader and a good follower are synonymous. It's like learning math: You have to complete algebra before trigonometry. Becoming a leader is something that you gain from embracing a solid following role. There is a common misconception that you are either a leader or a follower. Not true. The reality is that all leaders must also follow. Even a CEO must follow the leadership of their company's board of directors. Research has shown that the best leaders are also the best followers. Effective leadership and effective followership have much in common, but understanding how to follow can make you a better follower and a much better leader.

There is research that focuses on the follower in the leader-follower relationship. Two books, *The Art of Followership* by Riggio, Chalef and Blumen and *Followership* by Robert Kelley discuss this approach. Both of these books highlight how followers are creating change and making leaders better. There are different types of followers, just like there are different leadership styles.

Robert Kelley was the first to discuss different types of followers and the repercussions for leading them. "Sheep" is the term Kelley gives to followers who passively wait for leaders to give them directions or motivate them.

"Yes-persons" back their leaders, but still expect their leaders to make the decisions and to provide direction, before they are willing to move forward. The problem with yes-people is that they don't engage their brains or take initiative in moving the group or company forward.

"The alienated" are the followers who are independent, think they know what's best, and aren't afraid to challenge their leaders. Their skepticism and mistrust can create a lot of negativity within organizations.

"The pragmatics" watch out for themselves and back the leader they think will ultimately benefit them the most. Pragmatics like things the way they are and will defend the status quo.

It is the "star followers" that are the ideal, according to Kelley. Star followers are active, positive, and work with and for the leader to achieve good outcomes—and outcomes aligned with the direction and vision of the organization. Kelley describes them as "leaders in disguise."

Ira Chaleff also talks about these ideal followers in his book *The Courageous Follower: Standing Up to and For Our Leaders*. Courageous followers do everything possible to contribute to the leader's and the organization's success, but have the courage to constructively challenge the leader or the status quo if they think the direction is wrong. Importantly, the courageous follower helps prevent ethical abuses and misbehavior by the leader and others.

Noted leadership scholars Warren Bennis and James MacGregor Burns argue that effective followership is crucial for organizations and collectives to survive. Even the best leaders cannot be successful without courageous, "star" followers, and the qualities of these star followers are the same qualities possessed by the most effective leaders.

As an African American leader or team member (especially in corporate settings), you will find that opportunities are rare to follow successful, charismatic Black leaders. We are catching up, but still have a way to go when it comes to holding senior corporate leadership positions. It is vital that African American leaders set exemplary examples for their subordinates to follow whenever an opportunity presents itself.

Chapter 4

MENTORING AND LEADERSHIP

THE WORD "MENTORING" gets hurled around a lot in relation to leadership these days, and is sometimes, in my opinion, overused. However, mentoring is an essential part of leadership and the leadership development process. We all gravitate to those who possess great leadership abilities, and we often mimic their good traits. Conversely, we avoid the poor leadership traits we see in leaders who struggle. One-on-one mentoring is ideal, but not always available or necessary. I have learned a lot from watching and listening to leaders I have been exposed to, without having been mentored by them personally or one on one.

African American professionals can have a hard time developing mentoring relationships at times for various reasons. The lack of Black professionals in the workplace, unwillingness by some Black leaders to embrace or mentor their Black team members, and a complete lack of understanding of how important the mentoring relationship in the workplace is, are a few of the hurdles faced by

Black professionals and other workers seeking mentorship.

Rising Black professionals rarely see a large number of their peers in the workplace, compared to white professionals. During my military and corporate careers, I often found myself being the only African American on the team, or one of very few, which meant I had to figure a lot of things out on my own with regards to culture, office politics, socializing, and standards. Some will say being the only Black person on the team is no big deal, but until you have been in that position, you will never understand how difficult it can be at times. Your team members and your supervisor on occasion will either intentionally or unintentionally have preconceived notions or expectations about what you bring to the table, or how you fit in. Some will question if you even deserve to be on the team at all. Look at the racial discrimination lawsuits currently filed by Black IT professionals against tech companies in Silicon Valley.

Having a mentor, someone to demonstrate and voice how to navigate the landscape of the workplace, can be the difference between a mentee's failure or success. When I found myself in situations without a Black mentor (which was often), I relied on prior work experience, relationships, and interpersonal skills to survive, but not everyone possesses those things, especially early in their careers. Absent a mentor, it is important to be true to yourself and pay very close attention to happenings in the workplace. You should also embrace those who reach out to help you and share knowledge of your workplace with you, regardless of their skin color. As an African American leader, you have an obligation and should feel obligated to mentor up-and-coming aspiring Black professionals.

Unfortunately, there are a few Black leaders and professionals who want nothing to do with their Black team members. This behavior has been called self-loathing, crabs in a barrel syndrome… etc. Whatever you want to call it, it is very real, and I have seen it up close. I have experienced it a few times during my career, and it can be very frustrating. I once had a Black supervisor who felt uncomfortable talking to me one on one in the workplace. He told me that people would start to talk if they saw us talking to each other; it was almost like we were conspiring.

I found this very odd, because our white coworkers talked one on one all the time. This person would constantly look over their shoulder as if we were talking about something or someone important, when we would be just chatting casually.

Then there were my African American team members who immediately upon my arrival began to compete with me, creating a self-made competition between us, like there could only be one Black team member on the team. Both of the aforementioned were beyond perplexing!

I really don't know what causes this behavior, but I have always made an effort to embrace everyone in the workplace, especially my African American teammates, because I wanted to see them succeed. At times, some of my peers would accept my offers to mentor them, but there were those who were suspicious, like I was up to something or had an agenda. It is unfortunate that some Black people are conditioned not to trust each other and to be suspicious of each other, especially in the corporate world where we are so few.

While it would be ideal for a Black professional to have an African

American mentor, it is not an absolute must. Black leaders should seek out quality mentors regardless of race, because there are good leaders out there that will work with and mentor their team members equally, regardless of their skin color. I have had several mentors—some were white, some were Black, and they all greatly impacted my ability to become an effective leader and mentor. The big difference was that my African American mentors spoke to me from a perspective that my white mentors would never understand. That is why it is so important for African Americans in leadership positions to seek out young African Americans to mentor.

I've had countless mentors during my careers, and some of the best mentors I had were white. As executive director of a non-profit agency that mentored youth, I faced a shortage of mentors. At times, Black mentors did not step up to the plate, while many of our white mentors did. There were members on our board of directors that felt white mentors couldn't be effective mentors to Black boys. After doing some research and speaking with white mentors who had mentored Black boys, I discovered that the Black boys only cared about someone showing up and being there for them, not the color of their skin. I took the findings of my research and my conversations back to our Board of Directors and we reversed our thinking on whether white mentors would be allowed to mentor African American boys.

Mentoring is not about skin color; it is about helping a young person get to where they want to be in life. Black mentors are not always available or willing to help young Black professionals succeed in the business world or in the streets. In fact, I know of several successful Black leaders who refused to mentor or have anything to do with young Black professionals, for reasons I cannot explain.

One African American Army general did not have one Black officer on his staff, which is something all generals have control of, because they interview and select officers and NCO's to be on their staffs. Then there was a senior military officer, a friend of mine, who reached out to an African American executive for mentorship, only to be told his resume was horribly written, and that he was not entitled to any favors because they both were Black. My friend told me this conversation demoralized him.

African American Army generals and corporate executive leaders owe access to their knowledge and experiences to their Black teammates. Serving on those staffs is a form of mentoring that gives young officers and professionals access and connections that can benefit them for a lifetime. African American leaders have an obligation to pass on their knowledge to the next generation of young African American leaders. When you consider how rare it is to have a Black CEO leading a corporation or serve under a Black general in the military, it becomes even more important.

I mentored young African American males for over a decade, both inside and outside of the workplace. Young Black men are truly in severe need of mentoring. Many young African American men do not care about education, their appearance, or hard work. There is a void in our homes and communities. The void is fatherhood. Many of the young people I see struggling today were not given the tools they need to succeed in life: discipline, education, pride, dignity, self-love and self-respect. This does not apply to all young African Americans. There are young African Americans who are making major impacts in every aspect of society.

Black women are raising too many of our African American boys alone. They are doing the best they can, but they face tough challenges, especially when a boy becomes a teenager. There is a point in a young boy's life when he stops deferring to his mother as an authoritative figure. This is when a father or father figure is crucial. A woman cannot teach a boy certain things he needs to be a successful man, nor should any women have to. We as Black men must step up and help.

My work with nonprofit agencies showed me to how impactful mentoring in a young person's life can be, and the difference it can make. I have seen neglected, angry young men come into our programs and turn their lives completely around in a few years with the help and guidance of a positive mentors and role models. Unfortunately, there just aren't enough mentors available, but we can change this, call your local mentoring organizations or call the National Mentoring Resource Center

https://nationalmentoringresourcecenter.org.

Growing up, every adult male in my neighborhood was basically a mentor. They made sure we stayed out of trouble. They made sure we were behaving ourselves and they made sure we were always safe and well taken care of. Being looked out for and cared for is all a child needs to flourish. All children want someone to show them they care for them. I encourage anyone who has the time and resources to become a mentor to a child. Just a few hours a week can make a huge difference. Do it today. There is a young person out there who needs a mentor, who needs you. When we start mentoring our youth at an early age, we prepare them for a better and brighter future.

Army Brigadier General (Retired) Remo Butler wrote an article in the *Fayetteville Observer* several years ago about why Black officers in the military fail. The primary focus of the article was the lack of mentoring available to young African American officers.

Butler also highlighted that it was not always overt racism that caused some Black officers to fail, but rather a debilitating inertia in the way young Black officers were mentored and a lack of common cultural understanding amongst both Black and white officers.

I believe Butler's observations on mentoring also apply to corporate America and government employment as well. We tend to want to be around people we are comfortable with, and people who share the same views and values we do. This is human nature, but as leaders we must realize that embracing and accepting those who are different, and who don't always agree with us, can be a huge benefit to us as leaders.

There are talented people in the world who are different from us. As leaders it is vital that we acknowledge, nurture, and professionally develop those individuals regardless of their ethnicity. African American leaders must resist the urge to avoid their Black subordinates and peers in the workplace. We seem to be the only race of people who are doing this.

We must abandon the self-loathing and insecurities that are based on what we have been told about each other or our previous experiences. We need to give people a chance and trust each other. Appropriate professional development is the key to changing these mistrusting behaviors.

As leaders we must instill confidence in our team members, and we need to stress the importance of trusting and believing in others until they prove they are not worthy of that trust. We also need to be available and have compassion for our junior team members and let them know they are worthy and allow them to fail.

Mentoring is important to the development of all leaders, but it is vital for African American leaders to share their leadership challenges, struggles, failures, and successes with their African American team members. I owe a large part of my success to my many mentors and their patience while mentoring me. I have made it a top priority to mentor others, as share as much as I can especially with young African Americans.

An African American leader should never avoid and always embrace their responsibility to develop and mentor their team members. That means all team members, not just the ones they are comfortable with. Additionally, African American leaders need to stop worrying about perceptions when it comes to developing and mentoring their fellow Black colleagues and team members. I never understood this behavior because other races groom and mentor each other all the time. It is perfectly okay and logical to help those who show leadership potential.

Chapter 5

Leadership Challenges

AFRICAN AMERICAN LEADERS are increasingly emerging in the military, government, and the public and private business sectors. America has even had an African American president. Despite the increase in African American leadership, there are substantial leadership challenges for us that remain. In the public sector, election results at every level indicate that significant numbers of non-Black Americans remain reluctant to vote for an African American political candidate, irrespective of the candidate's qualifications or their positions on key issues. In the private sector, Joint Center research shows that, while younger Black professionals are more optimistic than their elders, a large majority of Black professionals believes that strong anti-discrimination laws (like affirmative action) and enforcement remain necessary because many CEOs and senior business executives express little concern about racial discrimination in their organizations. Many Black professionals feel corporate America remains a fairly hostile environment and racial discrimination is still a widespread problem, with tech companies being some of the reported worst offenders.

Why do Black leaders struggle? Opinions on this vary, from a lack of mentors and training, to communication skills, and lack of preparedness. There are also self-induced pressures, exclusion, and the fear of failing. Being an effective leader is impossible if you don't have access to opportunities and the proper training. An effective leader also requires access to good mentors, social events, key meetings, and discussions their superiors take part in. Self-sabotage is another cause of struggle for African American leaders. Self-sabotage comes by way of turning down opportunities for advancement, paranoia, and a lack of trust in superiors, peers, and teammates, especially their fellow Black team members.

Readiness, exclusion, unrealistic and perceived expectations, negative stereotypes, and lack of access and training are also key factors in why Black leaders struggle. My experiences revealed that some individuals who worked for Black leaders didn't give them the same amount of respect they gave their white colleagues. I'm not certain of the reasons for this behavior; however, I believe the history of how Black people came to America, and the negative stereotypes that have been perpetuated throughout time, impact how Black leaders (and other people of color in general) are perceived and how they are treated by their peers and subordinates. Being an African American leader comes with a lot of pressure and requires extreme patience, and you must be very thick skinned.

Black leaders still lag behind other ethnic groups in senior and leadership positions at corporations, institutions, and in government and the military. Unfortunately, some Black leaders who are in leadership roles in these organizations refuse to advise, or in some cases want anything to do with their Black teammates, almost ensuring those team members won't have access to critical training and mentorship required for them to advance and eventually be their replacements.

I observed and experienced both of the aforementioned during my career. I watched Black military officers who were afforded leadership opportunities refuse to offer their Black team members those same opportunities. On one occasion a friend of mine sent his resume to a Black general officer for review and constructive feedback, only to be ridiculed and chastised by the general. My friend was so hurt by the general's comments that he cried. During my military career, I attempted to seek out guidance from two senior SOF African American military officers. Both blew me off and refused to have any discussions with me about their careers or experiences as Black military leaders.

The lack of leadership training is another area of concern for many Black leaders. This comes by way of not having or being denied access to training, as well as being treated differently or excluded while attending such training. I experienced both during my career. I was denied opportunities to attend training on several occasions, which directly impacted promotions and advancement. Fortunately, I was able to overcome them.

I also attended training where I was excluded from after class study groups, evening social gatherings, and not afforded the same instruction, patience, encouragement and advice from course instructors that my classmates received. I had to work extra hard to keep up and finish course work and figure out a lot of things on my own. My career turned out fine because of my determination, but I know many Blacks whose careers did turn out well because of this type of behavior. African Americans should expect to have to work harder with very little help when attending leadership and advancement training, because there will be some instructors and classmates that don't think you belong there, which is very sad and unfortunate.

Confidence and Communication: I believe a lack of confidence and effective communication are among the top issues facing Black leaders today. Communicating effectively as a leader requires a great deal of confidence; if you are a leader without confidence, one of the first places it will show is in how you communicate with your team members. Leaders who lack confidence regularly second-guess their decisions. Technical competence is vital to communicating effectively. Knowing your job, what you are talking about, and being able to effectively relay that knowledge to others is important for any leader. People will not follow or respect an incompetent leader who doesn't communicate effectively.

During my career I worked for Black leaders who struggled mightily with communicating effectively. When challenged or frustrated they would yell, curse, and pull rank when they felt their authority was being challenged. Many times, these leaders weren't being challenged, but were simply being asked to clarify, or restate their position or the directions they had given to their team members. Losing your composure, yelling, or reminding people you are in charge doesn't gain a leader respect. Whenever you are challenged or someone is being insubordinate, think about how a calm person would handle the situation.

Preparedness is a key element that goes hand in hand with confidence. Black leaders must be overprepared and work harder than their peers. Leaders who are not prepared to lead can have a negative impact on everyone in the organization. Being prepared consists of continuous planning, organizing, training, equipping, exercising, evaluating, and taking corrective action. Meticulous record keeping and staying alert and engaged in meetings is also vital to being prepared.

Having confidence and being able to effectively communicate are fundamental to being an effective leader. Clearly and confidently relaying your message and your vision to your team can be the difference between failure and success and calmness or chaos inside your organization.

Exclusion: Having access to effective leadership, training, and having a seat at the leadership table are vital for a leader's success. Black leaders are at times excluded from some of the most important meetings and social events where major policies are being discussed and important decisions are being made.

Young executives and military officers will likely learn from and mimic leadership styles they are exposed to early on in their careers. The more they are exposed to senior leaders, the better the odds are that they will be successful as leaders themselves. Black leaders must make an effort to attend as many meetings and functions as possible. If you are not invited, ask for an invite. A person cannot learn or be an effective member of the team if they are unaware of the inner workings of and what is important to their organization. Meetings, social events, and through written and oral communications is where these important decisions are made. Let your leaders know being included in these events is important to you.

Conflict: All leaders deal with organizational conflict, be it in-office quarreling, insubordination, peer competition, or gossip. As a leader, you should address organizational conflicts as soon as they become present in the workplace. Listen carefully to both sides fairly, and render a decision or course of action as soon as possible. Being prepared will allow you to address conflict in a clear, concise manner.

Unfortunately dealing with turmoil and insubordination is all too common for Black leaders. Being prepared and having an understanding of human behavior helps but knowing the people you lead is more important. Understanding people and what moves and motivates them will help any leader regardless of race.

Young African American professionals today are more optimistic, self-confident, and confidently leaning toward corporate America than their predecessors. Some, however, have their optimism replaced by cynicism and disappointment as they experience disappointment due to racial inequalities and other negative experiences in corporate America.

Leadership poses a host of challenges that are not exclusive to Black leaders; however, Black leaders face additional scrutiny and more severe outcomes if they do not handle those challenges effectively. I have found the best way to deal with any challenge is to address it immediately and provide a solid course of action to mitigate the loss of morale and organizational effectiveness. Black leaders need to understand that the standard will always be higher for them in terms of performance... there's a certain benefit of the doubt given to white leaders when it comes to how much rope they are given with regards to making mistakes within their organizations.

Chapter 6

Compassion and Leadership

Compassion is an essential character trait that effective leaders possess. Compassion is a sense of concern for the suffering of others, but more importantly, it's the desire to see that suffering end. Being a compassionate leader doesn't mean that you are responsible for your team members' problems, but leaders do need to listen, show concern, and assist our team members if we can. During my career, I worked for leaders who lacked compassion, and I watched morale and productivity decline because of it.

I worked under leaders who showed compassion for their team members, and those few who completely lacked compassion altogether. Unfortunately, those leaders who lacked compassion vastly outnumbered those who displayed it. Having compassion is important to many parts of our lives, and I believe it is crucial for leaders, and those who are responsible for caring for and developing others, to show compassion. Early on during my military career, there was a culture which taught that having compassion as a leader made you weak and ineffective. The motto often heard was "suck it up," which essentially meant, "Don't complain regardless of the circumstances, and leave your private or personal issues at home."

Countless senior officers and enlisted leaders concealed their personal family troubles, relationship problems, and medical and other personal issues for fear of them being revealed to their leadership, because they thought it would make them look weak or cost them promotions and consideration for higher leadership positions. Subsequently, this behavior made those leaders' team members feel they had no choice but to hide their personal problems too, which many times were much worse than their leaders' problems due to their status and lack of military experience and resources.

During my military career, I concealed personal family and medical issues on many occasions because I thought if I told anyone about them, I would be disqualified for promotion, or that it would be held against me at some point later on in my career. There was this perception that a person who couldn't manage their personal life had no business leading others, which I now know is pure nonsense, but at the time I believed it. Unfortunately, this mindset still permeates in certain military and corporate organizations today.

The military is different in many ways from civilian and corporate life, but both are very competitive, and competition brings with it a certain amount of stress, uncertainty, and a lack of caring.

Competition sparks mean streaks amongst peers that makes them do things they normally wouldn't do to get ahead. Believing and feeling like your leadership doesn't care or want to hear about your personal issues or concerns leads to low morale in the workplace and can sometimes leads to tragic consequences for team members.

Compassionless leaders fail to see situations through their subordinates' eyes, and to understand what is important to them. I have worked for leaders who lacked compassion. I served under a senior military officer who thought people who took time off to be with their families were weak and uncommitted to the mission. He created a culture where everyone worked themselves to death and abandoned their families. Morale in that organization hit an all-time low due to high divorce rates.

I have observed many instances where team members were mentally, socially, and sometimes physically abused due to a lack of compassionate leadership. In most of those cases, the individuals on the other end of this abuse were different from their leaders or were going through personal struggles. In every one of those cases, none of the individuals deserved to be treated the way they were treated. Effective leaders don't bully their team members.

Showing compassion as a leader creates a positive work environment that can produce amazing results. We invest so much in our businesses, but we don't invest in our most important assets: our people. When your team members know you care about them, they will go above and beyond. They will buy in to your vision and take pride in your brand.

I have had the privilege of leading hundreds of men and women, both in the military and private sectors, and I didn't always lead with compassion, but I have seen the positive results and personally witnessed what happens when you show the people who work for you that you care about them. By showing your team members compassion, you can become a better, more effective leader.

Compassionate leaders are effective leaders; they understand the impact of their words and their deeds. They use the word we instead of I, they create great work environments, and they inspire, empower, and connect with their team members.

Chapter 7

Developing Teammates

Developing team members is an important task for any leader, regardless of their race. How do you get team members to do things the right way, your organization's way, and motivate them to buy in to your leadership vision, and your brand? You start by establishing a very high standard and setting a great example from the outset. This is accomplished by having confidence in yourself, your abilities, and leading by example. They are critical to your teammates' development. Leading by example means quite simply showing your subordinates how to do their jobs effectively and how to carry themselves and conduct themselves in the workplace at all times.

Successful teammate development requires a leader to be professional in appearance and professional in words and performance. As leaders, we don't always get to choose our team members. Sometimes we are intentionally and unintentionally given team members that presents us with a challenge. That is why establishing standards first thing is so important.

Providing new team members an effective and thorough in briefing when they arrive to work for you is one of the most important parts of their professional development. This is the leader's opportunity to ensure the new team member succeeds. Do not pass this responsibility off to anyone else; conduct the initial brief yourself.

The initial brief a team member receives from their leadership can set them up for success. By letting them know your values, expectations, and what they need to do to be successful, you take the responsibility for making sure that new teammates understand what is required and expected of them and what is not tolerated in the workplace. I also believe it is helpful to have a written organizational mission and vision statement for teammates to visualize and comprehend.

As an African American leader, you will be assigned team members who may have never had a Black supervisor or have never taken orders from a Black person. You may also have newly assigned personnel who have more work experience or may be older and more educated than you are. This happens in corporate America.

This is where a leader's self-confidence, preparation, and experience are most required. During my career, there were members on my team who were more educated and experienced than me. However, I didn't view those individuals as a threat; I viewed them as valuable team members and assets. I regularly sought their input and had discussions with them about their experiences. I could tell they appreciated it.

It is extremely important for a leader to take care of the members of their team. When you take care of your people, and you are competent and professional, everything else will tend to take care of itself. On occasion during my career, I had team members alert me that someone on the team was trying to undermine me. All leaders deal with this; unfortunately, Black leaders deal with it more than others. I have seen this happen many, many times over the years.

The reason those teammates told me about the disloyalty of their team member was because they knew I cared about them and they wanted me to succeed. It is vital for leaders to build a work environment where it's hard for dissension to survive. Effective leadership can prevent and decrease disharmony in the workplace. There will on occasion be someone on your team that will attempt to disrupt harmony and divide the team.

During an assignment in South Korea, a soldier who worked for me constantly spread negative gossip about what I was doing as a leader. Unbeknownst to him, some of his team members were coming to me and telling me what he was saying. Having this information allowed me to counter his negative attacks and frustrate him, because I was always one step ahead of him.

The soldiers came to me with the information because I took care of them all and I was fair and compassionate as a leader. My team members knew the things this soldier was saying weren't true, and they were happy with the way I was leading them. Now, had I given them reason to believe the negative gossip, it would have been a different story. In the end, my team members didn't believe the negative rumors because they knew better.

There is a lot more to developing team members than dealing

with and managing conflict. As leaders, it is very important that we remember how things were for us when we started our careers. Too many leaders attempt to put their team members through hardships just because they (the leader) experienced hardships early on in their own careers.

Leaders should remember the hard lessons and experiences they had and do everything in their power to ensure that the team members they are now responsible for have better experiences at the beginning of their careers. We should always try to make things better for our team members.

One of the most important lessons and traits you can emphasize to your team members is to be punctual. This is the foundation to being productive and effective as a leader. You cannot do anything effectively if you are not on time for it. There has been tons of research done on the effects of tardiness in the workplace. Low morale, productivity, and millions of dollars are wasted in business due to individuals not being on time. One survey conducted in the UK found that over 9 billion dollars was lost due to people being tardy for work.

Punctuality was a problem for me early on in my career, but I quickly realized if I wanted to achieve success, I had to start managing my time better. I owe a large part of my success to being punctual and being early for everything. That means every event, both work and socially related. Showing up on time gives you an advantage over your peers. It gives you time to prepare and deal with problems if they exist, prior to your work shift starting.

When I talk to my friends who are business owners and executives, they all list being punctual as one of the most important traits they look for when selecting team members for pay raises, promotions, and other favorable actions in their businesses.

Appearance and professionalism are also very important. I have seen so many team members get passed over for promotions and pay raises and lose their jobs because of the way they looked or they way they acted on the job. African Americans really struggle with this, for reasons I don't understand. Conforming to business and professional attire and etiquette does not make you a sellout.

I was in a very popular coffee shop the other day and witnessed a young barista having a very loud conversation with two of her friends who were sitting at a table nearby. They were so loud I could hear them even with my headphones turned up. They were clearly bothering customers, but I decided not to say anything because I didn't want any confrontation. More importantly, it wasn't my job to say something; it was the manager's job. This was just one example, but I have witnessed many others.

Many years ago, I had to tell an African American co-worker that his behavior in the workplace was unprofessional. He immediately dismissed my comments and accused me of being self-loathing and jealous of him because he was more popular in our workplace than me.

When I explained to him that the people who he thought he was popular with were the same people calling him unprofessional and talking behind his back, he got mad and quit speaking to me. This is something Black leaders need to be prepared for when you correct or discipline your African American team members. Some will take it harder coming from you than if a white leader corrects or comments on their behavior.

Appearance is also very important in the workplace; we are being judged by others based on what we look like, especially our attire. The best way to show your team members what professionalism looks like is to set the example yourself. Team members will usually follow their leader's lead when it comes to attire and behavior in the workplace. Leading by example cannot be stressed enough.

A leader can be punctual, dress properly, and behave professionally, but if a leader is not technically proficient (knows their job) they may as well not show up at all. Technical proficiency is simply knowing and being very good at your job. Although all of the aforementioned are important, knowing your job is the most important.

I have seen leaders and team members with poor attitudes and bad behavior who were technically proficient be tolerated by their leaders. I have also seen team members with an unprofessional appearance be tolerated because they were technically proficient.

Leaders need to be precise when teaching their team members how to do their job. Clearly articulated standards and requirements must be established and adhered to. Leaders who deviate from established standards and procedures for any reason will soon see a decline in productivity and morale. There are many characteristics required to successfully develop team members, but punctuality, appearance and professionalism, and technical proficiency are the most important ones.

Leaders should always be evaluating, teaching and developing their team members. Leaders should also be constantly identifying and searching for those who have potential to be leaders, and those who can one day be their successors.

Chapter 8

LEADING UPWARD

LEADING UPWARD IS a concept about influencing your leaders, instead of constantly being led by those with more authority than you. Leading upward is not about being malicious or controlling your superiors; it is about improving productivity, processes, and relationships for both parties.

Regardless of your status at your job, you will likely have to report to someone higher up. Relationships with supervisors and senior executives can be very complex. Some leaders rely on a lot of input from team members, others do not consult team members at all, and some leaders use a combination of the two.

Understanding your boss's leadership style and how they prefer to communicate are keys to success when leading upwards. As a person in the trenches, you will likely be more of a subject matter expert (SME) on your specific duties. Your boss is focused on running an entire company. Being able to relay information to your boss in a way that garners trust and freedom for you to operate and do things to improve your work environment is vital.

When you consider that African Americans still lag far behind in holding leadership positions in most corporations today, leading upwards becomes more important as it relates to quality of life in the workplace for Black leaders and team members. That is why technical proficiency is so important. A supervisor will not allow anyone who doesn't know what they are doing to give them suggestions or rely on them as a SME.

Leading upward is about being skillful, competent, and most important, being a valuable member of your team. The history of African Americans in the workplace shows that they have historically contributed greatly to the success of their organizations without being in a leadership role.

The truth is that most leaders are looking for team members whom they can develop and groom for positions of greater responsibility. They look at those in the workplace who conduct themselves like leaders, even though they are not in charge. African Americans in business and in the workplace should embrace the challenge and opportunity to lead upward.

I have experienced being shut down by a supervisor or boss on several occasions. I went to them with what I thought was a great idea only to get shot down before I could go into detail. I have also been denied extensions on projects I was working on.

Initially, I thought my bosses were being difficult, but after analyzing each situation, I realized my presentation or communication was lacking in most cases. Being able to communicate persuasively and respectfully to get your point across to your leaders is a critical workplace skill that must be developed. That is why it is important to make an effort to understand your leaders if you want to be successful at leading upwards.

I believe leading upwards is one of the most important skills you can possess. To start leading upwards, you'll need to learn what is important to your supervisor and the organization, so that you can demonstrate how what you're doing or asking for is applicable to their top priorities. This is why it is also important to know more about your company than just the job you do daily. Knowing other components of the workplace and what your co-workers do is vital to leading upwards.

Be respectful, prepared, and well organized when approaching a supervisor with an idea or proposal for something you are working on. It also helps to be professional in appearance and attitude. Leaders are less likely to be receptive to ideas and suggestions if you are not prepared. Build strong relationships with your supervisors and team members. As people, we tend to be more willing to help those we like, so get friendlier with your teammates. You never know when a supervisor may ask them for input on your idea or proposal.

Chapter 9

NETWORKING FOR SUCCESS

NETWORKING IS ESSENTIAL to be an effective leader in the military and private sectors of business. The exchange of ideas and information amongst leaders in business and social settings provides leaders opportunities to learn from one another and share business-related best practices and failures. Networking also allows leaders to learn about one another on a personal level and learn about each other's backgrounds and family.

Leaders who network effectively have more success than those who don't. Networking is not sucking up. There is a misguided perception amongst some African Americans that if you have influential, or white, friends and business associates that you are a sellout or have sold out. This is the farthest thing from the truth.

There is nothing wrong with making friends and connecting with people you like, or need to learn from. There is also nothing wrong with sharing experiences and maintaining contact through social events, social media, and personal contact to help each other have success in business and in life.

During my career, I made it a priority to engage with my leaders, peers, and those who worked for me, mainly because I am genuinely interested in people and their stories, but also because you never know who you're amongst in the workplace.

During my first tour at Fort Bragg, I had a soldier named Keith who had a master's degree and a father who was a millionaire. This kid was very smart and somewhat intimidating. After sitting and talking with him, I learned he was serving in the Army to gain leadership experience to take over his father's business. Keith became a person I would go to for advice even though I was a staff sergeant, and he was a private first class. I learned it was important to get to know everyone who works for you, from my experiences with Keith.

Social events are a key fabric of business and leadership. There are many leaders who lose opportunities because they fail to see how important it is to go out and have a beer with the team. How a leader handles himself or herself in social settings is a part of how leaders are evaluated. I have witnessed several rising stars lose opportunities because they refused to attend team-sponsored social events or because when they did attend, they couldn't hold their liquor.

One of my neighbors years ago, a young black captain in the 82nd Airborne Division, had a wife who refused to attend unit social functions and wanted to withdraw from the Family Support Group, which for commissioned officers is a kiss of death. My wife and I explained to her that as a commander's wife she had an obligation to the soldiers under her husband's command and their families. We also explained how important it was for her to make a good impression with the senior commanders' wives to help her husband's career. Eventually she became more comfortable with her role and became fully engaged. Our neighbors were fortunate to have a senior enlisted person living near them to provide guidance and share valuable career information.

Networking is about building trusting and long-lasting relationships that may be able to benefit you now and in the future. As a sergeant major, I worked with many young captains and majors. I always tried to treat them with respect and share information with them if I could, regardless of their age or military rank. Many of those captains and majors are now generals or retired generals. Networking is not about only building relationships with your superiors; it's about building long-lasting, trusting relationships with everyone you encounter in the workplace.

Chapter 10

LEADING FUTURE GENERATIONS

FROM MY OPTIC, this is one of the major challenges for all leaders. With technology providing expedient and non-linear communications in the workplace, a different value system and the age gap between today's senior leaders and their youngest team members, leaders will have to make adjustments to their standard leadership and team development practices to be effective.

I do not believe a leader can truly be effective in today's business climate if they don't embrace technology, especially social media. Today's youth are greatly influenced by social media platforms and they use them as a primary way of communicating. Social media is also one of the key means to make a "call to action." Everything from fundraising and activism to disaster relief uses these platforms to bring awareness and reach the masses in a short amount of time.

Learning to communicate via social media platforms is vital for all leaders. I worked for a fitness center director who refused to use or engage our members via social media. The director seemed proud to be a nonuser of social media, almost as if something was wrong with people who did use these platforms. They did not realize they were in the minority, and that social media engagement could boost memberships. The entire staff developed this anti-social media mentality, which caused the fitness center to struggle with relevance, and more importantly, sales and new memberships.

Social media is not the only technology that is important to leading the next generation. Effective personal engagement is the best way to better understand younger team members and what is important to them.

The new generation who is joining the job market for the first time is very different from the baby boomers or even the millennials. They care more about having a sense of purpose and having a positive impact on society and the environment.

According to the most recent Global Shapers Survey report, which featured the views of 30,000 people aged 18 to 35, young people feel they are perceived as lazy, impatient, and entitled and, as they are known as the "job-hopping generation," care little for work. The data, however, shows a different picture: the top two most important considerations for young people when considering job opportunities are "salary/financial compensation" and "sense of purpose/impact on society."

I attended a youth engagement forum at NC State University. The purpose of this forum was to get a better understanding of young people and what their priorities were. I attended because I was very interested in knowing what was important to them. As leaders, it is important to make an effort to understand the people you are teamed with.

The results of this forum were very enlightening. A youth panel of very impressive young people all stated that they liked a work environment that allowed them to be creative, and unrestricted when it comes to the physical environment. They stated they did not want to be tied to a cubicle for the rest of their lives.

I walked away from the forum enlightened and hopeful, because the young leaders at this forum were focused and driven. I also realized that I would have to make an effort to reach out to and better understand the young people I work with and those in my family. My biggest take away was I needed to be a better listener, especially to younger team members, because we have a tendency to dismiss them.

As leaders, we need to allot the appropriate amount of time to developing and managing our teams. We also need to understand that today's workplace requires us as leaders to be decisive and create safe and compassionate work environments. We need to provide our team members honest feedback as soon as it is required. Below-standard performance or improper behavior should be addressed and corrected immediately. Addressing these issues when they happen helps teammates realize their shortcomings and prepares them to be better leaders in the future. Lastly, listen to and respect your young team members and remember you were once in their shoes, learning and trying to find your way.

Chapter 11

THE ONLY BLACK IN THE OFFICE

BEING THE ONLY African American in a work environment (especially corporate) can be challenging and intimidating. If you are in that position, it means you are capable, have potential, you were given an opportunity, and you belong. I was the only Black, or one of a few, for a large part of my military career while serving in Special Operations. I personally experienced the anxiety and pressure of being the only Black, knowing that I had very little room for error and that I would be judged differently. Corporate America still severely lacks in diversity; there are currently only four Black CEOs at Americas Fortune 500 companies.

During my career, I experienced racism, passive aggression, exclusion, and being overlooked for advancement. There were occasions when I arrived at business meetings where I was asked was I sure I was at the right place? I do want to stress that in most cases the aforementioned incidents occurred sparingly; however, it didn't make them any less humiliating. I took a lot of pride in representing myself well and proving people wrong, which meant I had to overprepare and work twice as hard as most of my teammates.

Every experience I had as the only Black in the office wasn't negative. I had great experiences and a lot of fun as well, because I understood and embraced my environments, was very confident, and I felt I brought something to the table. A big part of being successful regardless of your race is having confidence, being competent, and being prepared.

Below are a few tips that helped me to survive and occasionally excel as the only Black in the office. I am sharing them with hopes that they will help you if you find yourself in that situation.

1. Earn Respect: Earning your teammates' respect is done by being professional in every way and setting a positive image and tone from the outset. You only get one chance to make a first impression. This sounds simple enough, but if you show up acting and dressed unprofessionally, no one will respect you. Watch what you say and be careful when playing around with co-workers. Never allow anyone to make racially sensitive or sexually explicit comments to you, even in jest. If you allow it once, you have signed up for it to happen over and over again. Your boss and co-workers' respect is something you have to earn if you are going to be successful.

2. Be Punctual: That's right; we have all heard the jokes about Black people being late for everything. This is no laughing matter; no one wants a teammate who is not dependable, and no employer wants an employee who is habitually late. Showing up early for work gives you an advantage over those who don't. Most occupations require some preparation before the workday

starts. From starting a shift as a server in a restaurant, to running your own company, showing up early gives you the opportunity to prepare and be ready to go when it's show time.

3. Lose the Attitude: You were hired because management saw something in you. You do not have to be aggressive and intimidating to everyone in the office to prove your worth. You and your co-workers are equal; you only have to prove yourself to your boss. I have seen some Blacks automatically assume they are under attack, or that they must prove something to everyone in the office. I felt this way when I first entered the white-collar work force too. Please give your co-workers the benefit of the doubt until they prove you wrong. There is no need to create beef where there is none. Avoid being thin-skinned, sensitive, and emotional about things, and avoid contentious conversations, especially about politics and religion.

4. Work Hard and Seek Improvement: I really don't know when the stigma of being lazy became associated with Black people, but it permeates throughout the workplace. Considering America was largely built on Black labor, it is absolutely absurd that many Americans still feel this way. As the only Black worker in the office, you will definitely receive scrutiny. Work hard, find a mentor, ask questions, seek improvement, and show interest in your work. A mentor can be a big help with getting you acclimated and can assist you with your transition.

5. Be Yourself: When a company interviews you, they are looking for the right person and the right fit. If they select you, that means they feel you are the right person for them. I have seen Black co-workers morph into someone else once they

are hired, to fit in and be accepted by their white coworkers. Don't do this! I once had a Black co-worker start riding Harley Davidsons, dipping tobacco, and listening to country music to fit in. Everyone laughed at him behind his back! Like I said earlier: You were hired because of what you as an individual brought to the company. Don't try to become someone else just to fit in.

My experiences as the only Black in the office have been mostly positive because of my attitude and my desire to succeed. Most people in the workplace (supervisors and coworkers) only care about productivity and the bottom line. When you do your job and work hard, your co-workers will eventually look past your skin color and begin to value you as an important member of the team. There will always be some people that will never accept or want anything to do with you, and that's okay. You are better off without them, and you will still have opportunities to be successful like everyone else.

There is no way to explain being the only African American in the office; you have to experience it, and I am sure the experience is different for everyone. For me, it was an interesting experience that I embraced. I knew I was always being watched and judged differently than everyone else. I also knew that I was somehow a representative for my race, which is usually what happens regardless.

It takes a strong-willed Black person to navigate their way through and be successful in the corporate world. However, with the right preparation and attitude, it can be a positive, rewarding experience.

Chapter 12

Effective Communication

Effective communication is arguably one of the most important traits a leader must possess. Communications skills are required regardless of race, but as an African American leader there is more involved than stating what is required or stating your intentions. African American leaders must occasionally restate their position or guidance more than once. I have had to do so on several occasions. It was almost as if the members of my team were checking to see if I was sure of what I was saying.

There are also diction and dialect differences that we can't ignore. There are several traits needed to be an effective communicator, regardless of your ethnicity. You have to be confident and competent. I recall a senior military official who consistently miscommunicated his intentions and desires, which caused a lot of chaos for his staff. On one occasion, his staff worked on a project for three months; when presented with the results, the officer said it was not what he ordered the staff to do. A vast number of resources and time were wasted because of his ineffective communication.

Written communications are the way we communicate the majority of the time in the current work environment. As leaders, it is very important that we express ourselves precisely when we communicate in writing—both email, text, and official written correspondence.

Most of the problems with communications in business today stem from poorly written emails, text, and official correspondence. Leaders make assumptions, or they don't proofread their correspondence before hitting send. We don't have to hit send on electronic communications until we are ready.

During my time in the military and corporate sectors, I witnessed countless examples of leaders failing to effectively communicate in writing. My rule is that anything you write should be able to stand on its own without any further explanation or without you being present. When your written communication requires additional explanations or clarifications, it is not an effective communication.

Communicating effectively in meetings is also crucial for effective leaders. This means communicating before, during, and after the meeting ends. I have attended numerous meetings over the years that lacked purpose, organization, focus, or any type of direction. Those meetings wound up wasting everyone's time, but more importantly, they didn't produce any results. I have also left meetings where all of the attendees were confused but no one asked for clarification during the meeting. Leaders must encourage feedback from their team during meetings.

The key to leading effective meetings is to establish an agenda, establish a beginning and end time (and stick to them), invite the right people, and facilitate to keep everyone on track. There are other important elements to running effective meetings, but the aforementioned are the most important.

Government leaders are notorious for scheduling purposeless meetings that waste people's time. Any leader who doesn't respect other people's time will quickly lose the respect of their team members. As a leader, you will keep team members waiting on occasion, usually due to outside circumstances. When this happens, a leader should always apologize to his staff, especially if the wait is a long one.

Over the years I have worked for several leaders who regularly called impromptu meetings and video teleconferences. These meetings were almost always unorganized, lacking the right team members, and rarely produced any positive results, which meant we usually had to schedule subsequent meetings to achieve our goals. A leader who has respect for other people's time will be an effective leader. They will also be more productive and respected amongst their team members.

Video and streaming conferencing have become effective ways to conduct business meetings without having to go through the hassle of business travel. VTC's also allow leaders to assemble their teams quickly to resolve unexpected problems that arise. I have been using Zoom and other platforms for years before the recent pandemic.

Leading an effective video teleconference requires the same important elements required to run a regular meeting. The only difference is that there are etiquette requirements for VTC's that do not apply in meetings. Professionalism is required when it comes to attire, seating posture, and controlling your microphone. You should also avoid eating and horseplay when you are not on screen, because you just might (unknowingly) be on screen. It is also vital to send out the latest version of products (documents, PPT slides…etc.) to the entire team so everyone is getting the information they need and to ensure everyone is on the same page.

Today's leaders have multiple tools available to them to help them communicate more effectively and efficiently. This is why it is important to for leaders to embrace the latest technology and be informed on the latest trends. As leaders, we need to understand that technology doesn't revolve around us. Effective oral and written communications are the pillars of successful leadership.

Chapter 13

LEADERSHIP AND ACTIVISM

ACTIVISM IS PART of America's fabric. As an African American leader, it is nearly impossible to avoid addressing activism. The more responsibility you have and the higher position you hold will likely dictate you being drawn into activism or those types of discussions. Individuals and media outlets will seek your opinion on relevant and sensitive topics. In 2015, I wrote an article about avoiding altercations with the police, which is still unfortunately a hot topic nationwide today, especially with the events that took place in America in 2020.

The 2015 article got nationwide attention, and I was interviewed by multiple media sources. Some of the interviewers wanted me to be an activist against the police, while other interviewers wanted me to be an advocate for the police. My focus then was on solutions to avoid Black men getting into altercations with police, so I remained neutral, which made interviewers on both sides very angry and frustrated with me. I didn't write that article to validate anyone's politics.

As a leader, you need to be very careful about spreading your personal and political views in the workplace. You can inadvertently cause a very stressful environment for your team members if they have different views on sensitive topics. We have all seen a rash of firings recently of CEO's and other leaders because of insensitive comments in interviews and through social media.

I have always believed that our views make us different from one another, not superior or inferior to each other. However, there are many Americans who don't feel this way. This is one of the reasons American politics are so divisive today. As a leader, it is vital to listen to every argument and be willing to change your point of view on occasion.

With the current political climate, leaders need to be careful how they respond to current events and how they opine on topics that are controversial. When a leader speaks on such topics, they are viewed as speaking for their company or organization, not as speaking for themselves, which can cause problems for the businesses they work for. We have seen this happen recently to several national brands.

African American leaders must watch their support for activism very carefully, especially for causes that have negativity (real or perceived) associated with them. This can be very tricky because as a Black man there have been many good causes, I have supported that were somewhat controversial. When this happened, I usually provided some type of financial support to them instead of voicing my support or openly supporting them.

As I previously stated, activism has been a part of America's fabric since we separated from Britain. From the civil rights and labor movements to women's suffrage, activism has shaped how we live our lives and has made a major impact on America's moral journey. As leaders we must be able to appropriately deal with and responsibly respond to activism as it impacts our team members and our organizations.

Chapter 14

Toxic Leadership

I wrestled with whether I should address toxic leadership in this book. After my experiences with toxic leaders throughout my career, and considering how prevalent toxic leadership is today, I decided the topic needed discussion. I first heard and read about toxic leadership in the Army in 2004.

Army Colonel George E. Reed wrote an article on the subject and titled it "Toxic Leadership." Colonel Reed examined and explained this leadership style and the repercussions from it. The article fascinated me because it outlined some of the leadership traits I had witnessed during my career.

The primary description of a toxic leader in Colonel Reed's article is: "Destructive leaders focused on short term mission accomplishment. They provide their superiors with impressive, articulate presentations and enthusiastic responses to missions. But they are unconcerned about, or oblivious to, staff or troop morale or climate. They are seen by subordinates as arrogant, self-serving, inflexible and petty."

I believe every leader starts out wanting to do the right thing, but pressure, power, greed, and fear overcome them and turns them into toxic leaders. Toxic leaders destroy everyone around them. They create work environments that are chaotic and that have low morale. During my career, there were two toxic leaders that really stood out. The first one was a commander who was a chaos junkie that created turmoil whenever things were running smoothly.

He would walk into a quiet office where everyone was working efficiently and ask for something that was almost impossible to produce on a very short timeline. This leader did this solely to disrupt synergy and create chaos in our office. He seemed to enjoy seeing everyone scrambling to meet his demands.

This leader was also very paranoid and distrustful of everyone who worked for him. I remember being called disloyal by him on several occasions when I disagreed with him or expressed an opinion that was different from his. The organization I served in at that time experienced an all-time low in morale and productivity under this commander.

Everyone in the organization spent all of their time trying to figure out what type of mood the commander was in. We also spent a lot of our time overexplaining routine things to him. On top of all of that this leader was a liar. Lying is a common theme with toxic leaders, because they are lying to themselves all the time by telling themselves they are great leaders. Toxic leaders are usually delusional, and they blame everyone but themselves for things that go wrong in the organizations they lead.

The second toxic leader I worked for was a staff officer serving as my division chief, who destroyed morale in our division in less than a year. This leader took away presentation opportunities for all of his junior officers. He personally conducted every briefing to our senior leadership himself. Even worse, he would have his team spend hours and hours preparing presentations, only to change them or redo them himself at the last minute. He was a perennial micromanager.

This officer was so toxic that two members of the team decided to leave the military because they were afraid they would have to serve under this leader in the future if they stayed in the military. His lack of trust of his team members and his delusional opinion of himself set us back for years after he departed. Toxic leaders always leave an organization worse than they found them.

I found that the best strategy to deal with toxic leadership is to document everything, and if possible, have other team members present when requirements for a project are being considered. This is vital because many times toxic leaders don't know what they want and will constantly change their requirements.

I also believe that you have to be confident and precise when dealing with toxic leaders. They prey on team members who lack self-confidence and are indecisive, or those they think are weak. Lastly, effective overcommunication is my favorite strategy in dealing with a toxic boss. Overcommunicating reassures them that you are following their guidance, while at the same time keeping yourself from being surprised by continuous changes to a project's requirements by a toxic leader.

As a team member, it is important to realize your boss's toxic behavior usually has nothing to do with you or your performance, and that the foundation for their toxic behavior was laid long before they knew you. If you find yourself in an unbearable toxic leadership environment, document events and report them to HR or whatever means for resolution are in place at your organization.

Chapter 15

THE TALKING POINTS LEADER

TALKING POINTS ARE words that are put together to state a position, counter a point or position, or to prepare someone for an upcoming meeting, briefing, or discussion. In my opinion, talking points are becoming too much of a crutch for leaders.

Many leaders are now going into important meetings and negotiations unprepared and uninformed because they are letting their staffs prepare talking points for them. These talking points are linear and usually written from the perspective of the person who prepared them, not the leader or person who will be speaking or leading the meeting.

An example of this occurred in 2017 when then CEO of United Airlines Oscar Munoz released a statement after a passenger was dragged off of a United Airlines flight. His first statement had no apology to a passenger who was captured on video being forcefully removed from the plane to make room for United Airlines crewmembers.

After public outrage, most via social media, Munoz issued a second statement with an apology, followed by media appearances, to repair the damage, but the damage had been done. This situation could have been handled differently had Munoz waited to gather all of the information before making a statement. I believe that had Munoz deliberately prepared, reviewed, and carefully thought out his response, there would have been less public outrage.

A big problem with talking points is that the persons using them are rarely deeper in subject knowledge than what's in the talking points paper before them, which causes leaders to stay with the talking points paper narrative and not stray from it for fear of getting tripped up or appearing to look uninformed.

Great leaders take the time to learn about subjects that are important to their businesses and their teams. They do not rely solely on their staffs to prepare talking points and notes to make them look smarter.

Great leaders also bring the right team members to meetings and are comfortable not being the person who is presenting or who knows subject matter. There is a trend where some leaders try to pick the brain of subject matter experts, then go into meetings portraying themselves as the subject matter expert. I recall an instance where a subject matter expert who was vital to getting a project approved was not allowed in the decision brief because there wasn't enough room for him. Important questions were asked by senior leadership, and no one could answer them because the expert was outside in the hallway!

There is a lot wrong with this trend, but most importantly, it destroys the morale of the person who did the research and dedicated their time to learn a skill, only to be pushed aside by a leader who wants to take the credit.

From politics, to clothing trends, style, and speech, everyone seems to be following or mimicking someone else. Even worse, we depend on social media, biased news media, and the opinions of thought leaders to frame our thoughts, morals, and opinions. Many Americans repeat narratives from media outlets as if they are our own thoughts and viewpoints, without regard for the truth.

African American leaders need to learn how to use their power to influence and empower their subordinates in an effective way. African Americans leaders face many challenges, from insubordination to different expectations and standards. However, being in a leadership position is a rewarding experience, and it allows us to help others and grow as individuals.

Chapter 16

LEADERSHIP AND SELF-CARE

SELF-CARE WASN'T A thing when I started my career. I wish it had been. When I enlisted in the military, there was a "suck it up" mentality, which meant no matter what your problems were or how you felt, you kept driving on and doing your job. This mentality still exists in many military and corporate organizations today, but not as much as it did before.

Self-care is important for every member of the team, but even more important for leaders. One of the most important things a leader can do is properly develop their department heads and teammates so they can function efficiently in their absence. This allows leaders to take vacations and spend time with their families. I served under a prominent military commander who never spent any time with his family and viewed teammates who wanted to spend time with theirs as weak and uncommitted. The divorce rate in our organization soared, because individuals were scared to even mention family problems if they were having them.

As a leader, it is important to have a life away from work. A hobby or just spending time with your family does wonders for your ability to lead. We all need to get away from time to time. Exercise is also a very important part of being an effective leader. Exercise allows you to release stress and helps with endurance and clarity for those tough decisions and long nights at the office. Exercise is also vital for your appearance.

Fortunately, nowadays there is more tolerance in the workplace for those who have personal and mental health issues. For the longest time, individuals dealing with this had to mask them or risk being ridiculed or even losing their jobs if the problems were discovered. However, recently we have seen people from politicians and actors to world-class athletes come forward to disclose their mental health issues.

As a leader, self-care is vital for you to be effective, and more importantly, take care of the team that works for you. This is why it is important to take vacations, get the proper amount of sleep, eat a healthy diet, take lunch breaks, use sick leave, and exercise regularly. Doing these things sets a great example for your team to follow, which will result in an increased atmosphere of positivity and will also likely result in increased productivity.

Self-care also applies to a leader's family. It is almost impossible to lead a team if you have issues at your household. We all deal with family issues and there is nothing wrong with that. However, ignoring those issues because of our leadership position does a disservice to our teammates and our families. Leadership requires you to accept your struggles and realize you're not weak for having them.

Leaders must observe their team members and look for signs of personal and professional issues they may have or are struggling with. Leaders should also create an environment where it is encouraged to come forward and seek help if problems do exist. Unfortunately, I have lost team members to suicide—team members who came to work everyday showing no signs of personal or professional troubles.

With the COVID-19 pandemic amongst us, 2020 was a year like no other in our lifetime. As a father, husband, personal fitness trainer, and small business owner, I have seen and heard countless stories of struggle, failure, and triumph from this past year. Going forward, looking out for ourselves and each other is crucial for our recovery, personal and professional growth, and well-being.

We must also accept and respect each other's differences. When we do this, we allow ourselves to learn about others and we allow ourselves to grow as leaders. Leaders cannot take care of their team members if they don't take care of themselves.

Summary

I have observed and been exposed to different and unusual leadership behavior as an African American leader. No matter how hard I tried to convince myself that some of the situations I found myself in were not racially motivated, deep down I realize that some of them were. African American leaders are held to a different standard, have different expectations, and are treated differently in many cases. That is the tax we have to pay. How we handle ourselves during these times can be the difference between succeeding and failing in business and in life. As Black leaders, we need to understand the circumstances and make adjustments regardless of our frustrations.

Throughout my career I watched African American leaders get passed over for leadership positions and promotions, and I saw a few get stripped of their dignity by the way they were treated. As an African American leader, you have to be tough, you have to be thick-skinned, and you have to understand that if you are put in a leadership position, you will be challenged and you will be tried. "Make those who try you wish they had tried someone else."

Many of the above-mentioned comments may be perceived as me having a chip on my shoulder, but as an African American leader, you have to have some type of an edge, and you have to be guarded to a certain degree. In most cases, the higher you climb up the leadership ladder and the more success you achieve, the more some people feel you don't belong there. It can be very taxing.

I expect there to be disagreements with my assessments about Black leaders, and that's okay. I am speaking solely from my experiences and observations during my service in the military and corporate sector as an African American leader.

I believe having an understanding and unique perspective of how Black leaders are perceived, how they are treated, and what they deal with gives you a distinct advantage and will allow you to better navigate through the leadership maze yourself.

I know several African American leaders who disregarded the things I talked about in this book. They felt they were being treated equal to their white peers. Most of them eventually experienced some type of unfair treatment, were passed over for promotion, or experienced other disappointments at some point during their careers

There are always exceptions and the possibility an African American in a leadership role may never experience any of the kinds of behavior I spoke about in this book. However, it is better to be prepared, because it is more likely you will experience some of these behaviors than not. The military, government, civilian, and corporate sectors have given me a unique opportunity to serve and observe leadership from a variety of perspectives.

Occasionally we are thrust into leadership roles without expectation or without pursuit. When this happens, you need to recognize that someone saw something in you and believed in you. Understand that you were selected for that role for a reason, and that you should lead with confidence.

There are so many definitions and variations of thought on leadership that this book can go on forever. I have attempted to address what I believe is the core of leadership, but effective leadership is something that is also determined by those who are being led.

I had up-close and occasionally personal access to some of the brightest minds in America. I learned a lot and I feel an obligation to share my experiences as an African American leader with current and future Black leaders. I hope you find something of value in this book that will help you as you travel on your leadership journey. I am grateful for my journey and blessed to be able to share it with you.

> "Learn to thrive outside of your comfort zone, because that is where you will spend most of your time."
>
> Matt Drayton

www.ingramcontent.com/pod-product-compliance
Lightning Source LLC
Chambersburg PA
CBHW070308230526
45470CB00002B/771